WHEN I GROW UP – I WANT TO BE
Copyright 2022 by Penelope Bunsen

All rights reserved. No part of this book may be used or reproduced in any manner whatsoever without written permission except in the case of brief quotations embodied in critical articles or reviews.

Thank you for purchasing the authorized edition of this book and for complying with copyright laws by not reproducing, scanning or distributing any part of it in any form without permission.
You are supporting the writers, illustrators and contributors for their hard work by doing this.
For information contact:
WIGUBK@TSproductions.org

For information about the When I Grow Up series of books
or to order these books in Chinese and Spanish,
Go to: Amazon.com
Written by Penelope Bunsen

Book ISBN: (978-1-7344435-2-3)
ePub ISBN: (978-1-7344435-3-0)
Printed in the United States of America.
First Edition Dec 2022

Hi! I'm Aralyn. I'm eight years old, and I live with my parents and my sister. I like to paint and color and to play with our bulldogs, Bruno and Ryder. Oh, and I also love to bake!

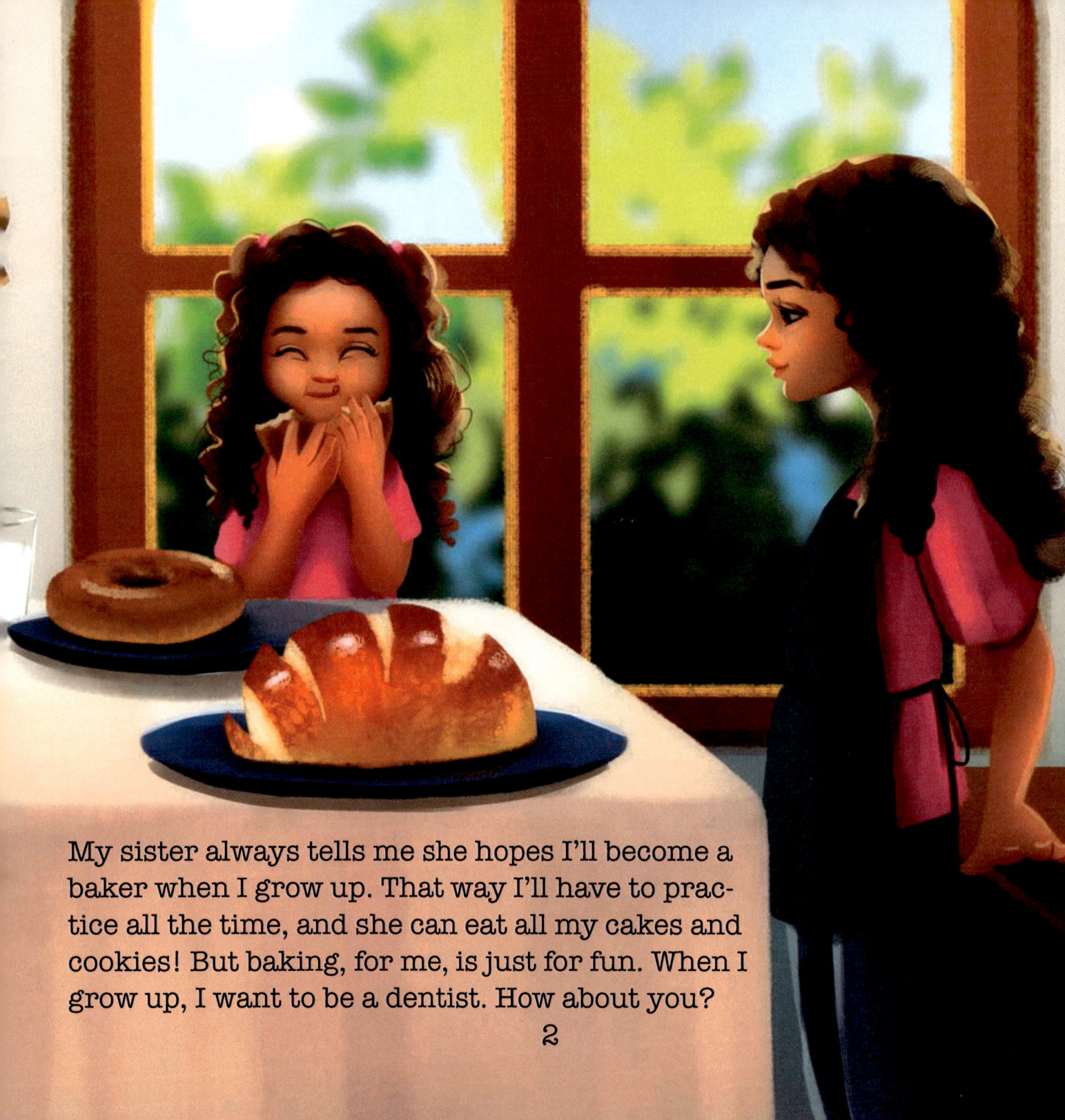

My sister always tells me she hopes I'll become a baker when I grow up. That way I'll have to practice all the time, and she can eat all my cakes and cookies! But baking, for me, is just for fun. When I grow up, I want to be a dentist. How about you?

Dentists help us keep our teeth strong and healthy, so we'll always have a beautiful smile and never get a toothache. Sometimes you have to be a little bit brave when you go to the dentist, but anyone can be brave. When you start to get scared, just think about something else. Something that you like. I think of unicorns!

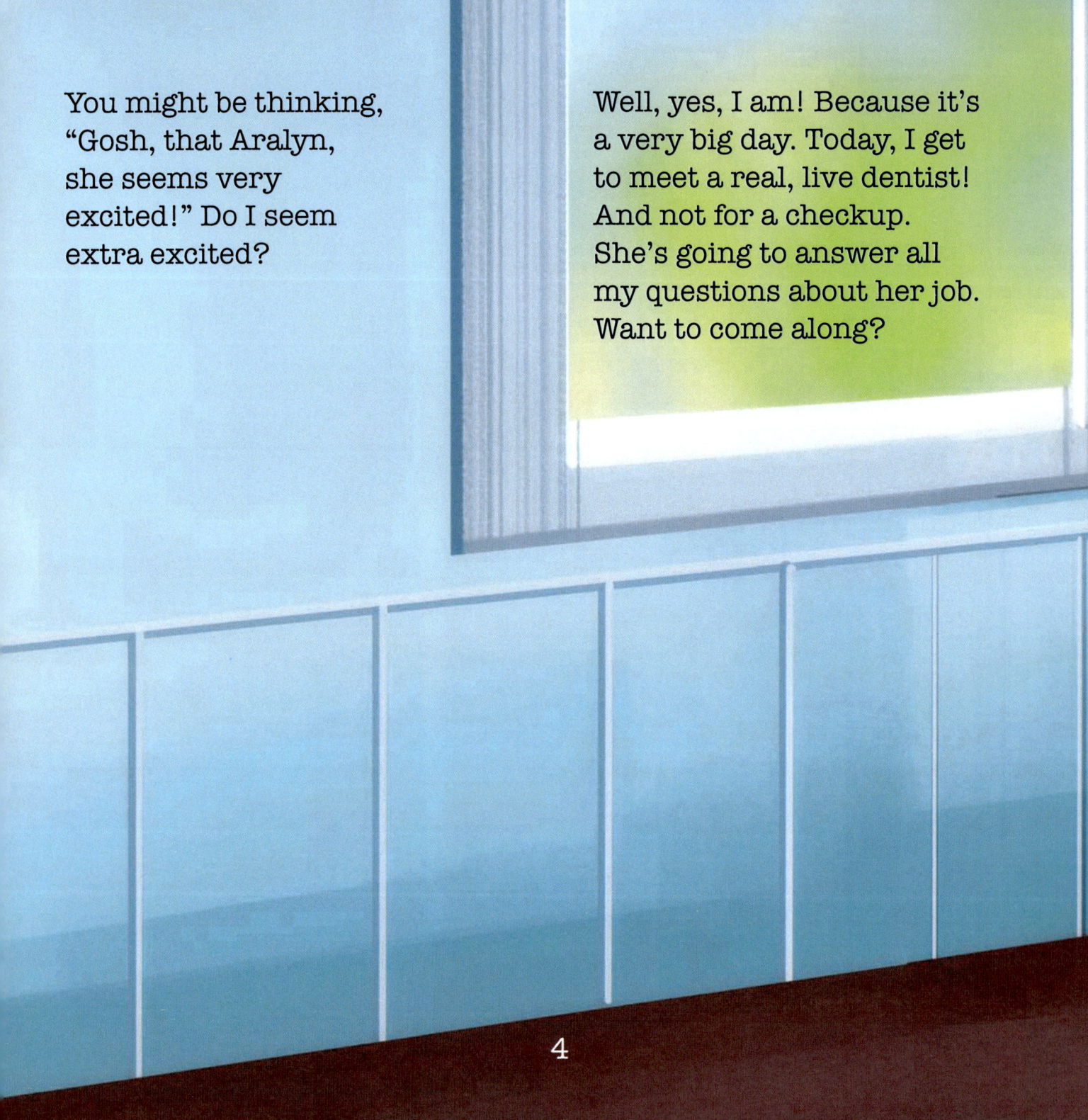

You might be thinking, "Gosh, that Aralyn, she seems very excited!" Do I seem extra excited?

Well, yes, I am! Because it's a very big day. Today, I get to meet a real, live dentist! And not for a checkup. She's going to answer all my questions about her job. Want to come along?

Interviewing an adult can be a bit scary. But we know how to be brave, don't we?

My sister says that when you're going to do a scary thing, it can help to practice it in advance. Want to help me? Here, let's pretend you're the dentist, and I'll practice asking you my questions.

Hi, Doctor! May I ask you a couple of questions?

Of course. Drill away!

Why did you want to become a dentist?

Because I wanted to let people know that dentists are nice and not scary at all.

How do you help kids stay calm when you're giving them a checkup?

I try to get them to talk about themselves, but sometimes it can be like pulling teeth! Maybe I need to brush up on my technique.

That was a great start! But you know what else is making me a little nervous? Talking to grownups. Especially grownups who have important jobs.

So, I asked my mom and dad what I need to know about professional interviews.

My mom said, *"Make sure you stand up straight, make eye contact, and don't interrupt the dentist when she's talking. And make sure you take your retainer out before asking questions."*

My dad said, "Let's practice a strong, grownup handshake. A good handshake helps you come across as serious and capable. Don't squeeze too hard, or you could break her fingers! But don't go too soft either."

All right! I think our interview is going to be clean and polished! We're ready to go to the dentist's office and meet Dr. Talin. Let's go!

Wow. Such a cool place. I'm so excited! And I love those plants. Oh goodness – I'm actually really nervous! But hey, I know what to do about that...

Hmm... I wonder if unicorns go to the dentist.

Well, I've practiced, I'm all dressed and ready to show how good a dentist I'll be, and I feel really prepared with my questions.

Here she comes!

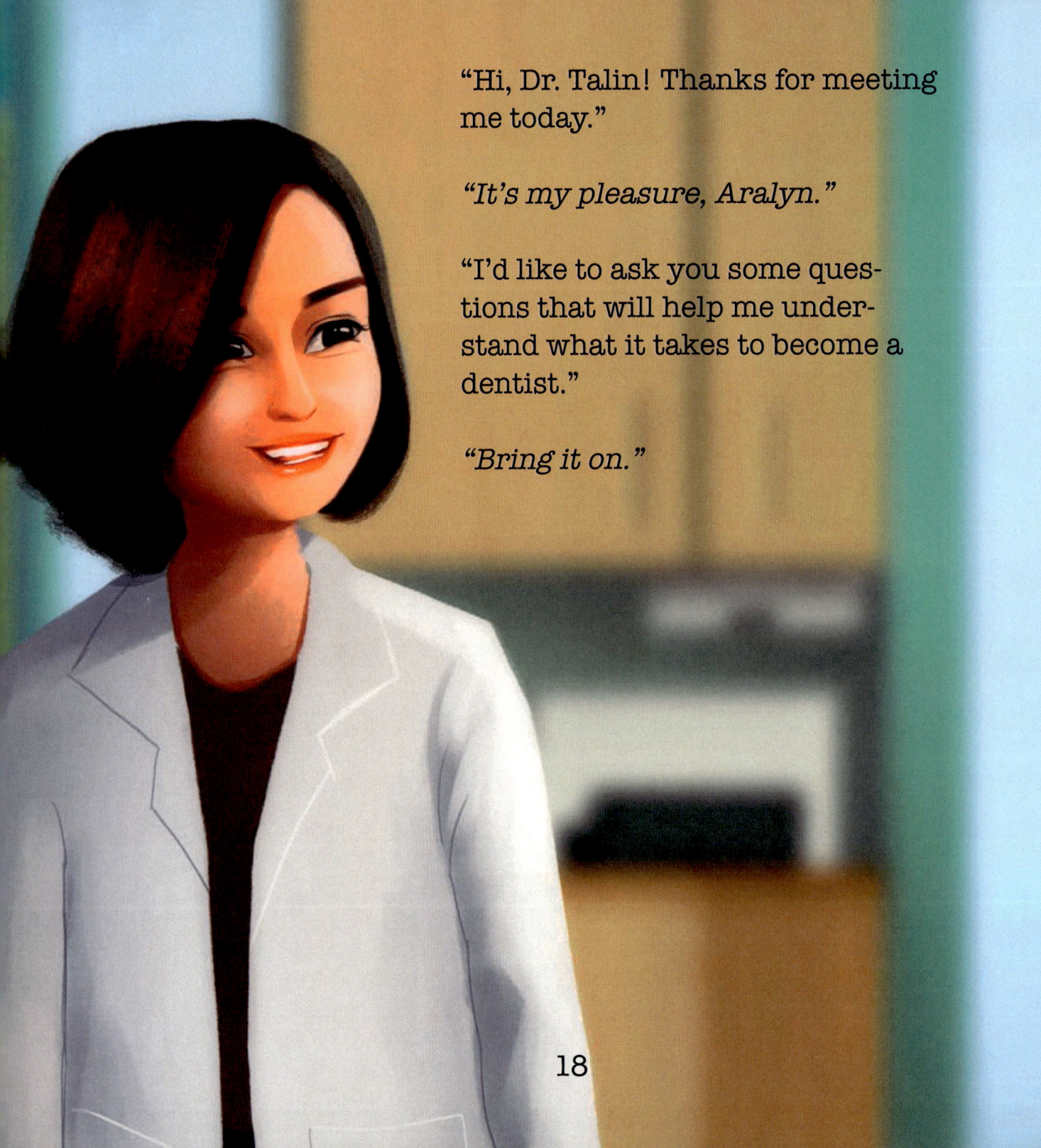

"Hi, Dr. Talin! Thanks for meeting me today."

"It's my pleasure, Aralyn."

"I'd like to ask you some questions that will help me understand what it takes to become a dentist."

"Bring it on."

"Why did you want to be a dentist?"

"Hmm... let me chew on that. Well, I've always liked helping people, especially children. I love making sure they have a bright smile and healthy teeth. That's why I like to do what I do."

"How long did you have to study to become a dentist?"

"After high school, I went to college for four years for a major in biology. And then I went to dental school, which was another four years. So it took me eight years all together."

"Wow, that's how old I am! That's a long time."

"It sounds like it, but it goes by quicker than you can say 'dental floss.'"

"How many people work at your office?"

"I have about twenty-five employees."

"Wow! You're in charge of a lot of people!"

"Half of them work in the front and half of them work in the back. The back is where we take care of teeth – cleaning them, taking X-rays – and the front staff handles the appointments and billing. Lots of computer stuff."

"Where do you work? Front or back?"

"I'm everywhere. That's why I wear sneakers. I'm the boss, so I've got to make sure I take care of the front staff and the back staff as well as my patients."

"Goodness!"

"But I like the back more, for sure."

"What is the hardest part of your job?"

"For me, it's to make sure everybody leaves happy and not crying."

"Crying? But you're so nice!"

"Well, some people are scared of the dentist and all the machines and the drilling and the scraping... especially the little ones."

That was when I decided I'd better think of unicorns again!

"What advice would you give a young person who wants to be a dentist?"

"Well, Aralyn, first make sure you take care of your own teeth really well. Brush twice a day for two minutes, floss, and eat healthy stuff, not candies, right?"

I laughed. "Um-humm!"

"Visit your dentist twice a year, and when you're at the office, ask lots of questions – like you're doing now! You can even ask them to show you what a cavity looks like on an X-ray."

"Oooh! Would you show me one? Can you show me an X-ray of a healthy tooth and a tooth with a cavity, so I can compare?"

"I absolutely can."

"I'm so excited."

"See here, the whiteish gray at the top, on the chewing surface? That's the enamel. Then the tooth becomes more of a cement gray? That's the dentin. And under that, where the gray is darker – like clouds when it's about to rain – that's the pulp."

"See how the tooth on the left has nice, clean layers, from lighter to darker, but the tooth on the right has some of that darker raincloud gray inside the lighter area? That's the cavity."

"Oh wow. That's pretty hard to spot."

"Don't worry, when you're in dental school, you'll get lots of practice!"

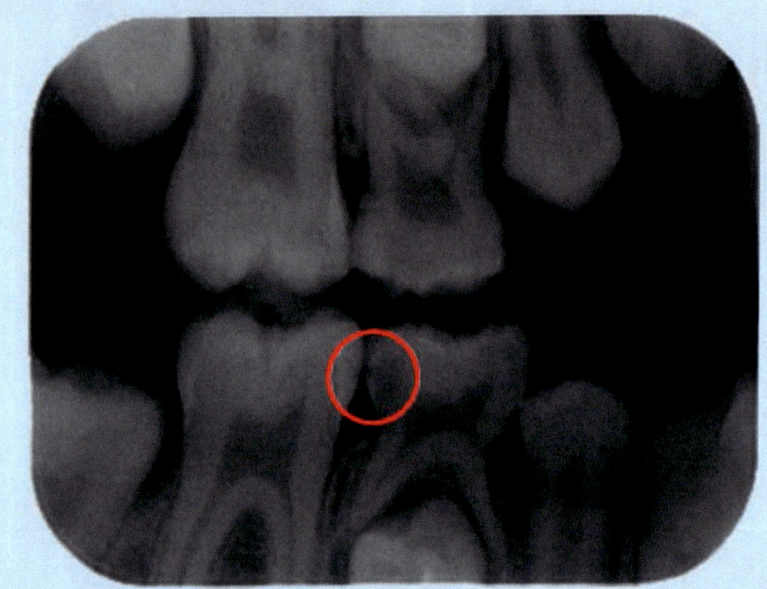

"Thank you so much for showing me, and for answering all of my questions!"

"You're very welcome, Aralyn. I love curious girls like you. Good luck in dental school! I'm sure you're going to do great."

"Me too."

That went so well! I got all the answers I was looking for. Thanks for practicing with me before. I think that really helped.

I'm so glad you could come with me for the interview. I hope you learned as much as I did! When it's your turn to interview a grownup, remember what we learned today: practice your questions in advance, stand up straight, and if you start to get nervous, just think of unicorns!

Thank you for joining me as I've learned all about what it takes to become a dentist when I grow up.

Stay curious, and don't forget to floss!

THANK YOU

I would love to thank Dr. Talin Janjik for her willingness to help this come to fruition and agreeing to mentor Aralyn in her quest to get answers for her future career.

CHILDREN'S DENTAL FUNZONE

1501 Colorado Blvd, Los Angeles, CA 90041
(323) 255-9663
https://childrensdentalfunzone.com/

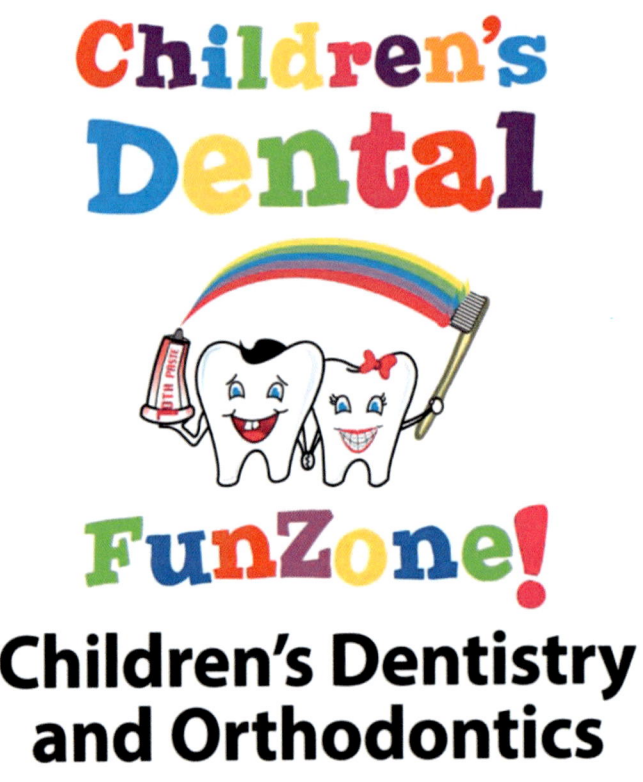

CREDITS

Writer

Penelope Bunsen

Editor

Stephanie Rosalyn Mitchell

Art Director

Gregory Van Zuyen

Assistant Editor

Phillip Lebovitz

Chinese Translator

Wen Hui Kuo

Spanish Translator

Autru Vich

Special Thank You to

Peter Bien

For addt'l Chinese review

Special thanks to Candice Cruz for being our host in the original format

Special thanks to my team.
Without them, this would not be possible.

Made in United States
Orlando, FL
15 August 2024